Jinny Johnson
Consultant: Steve Parker

First published in 2002 by
Miles Kelly Publishing Ltd
Bardfield Centre, Great Bardfield, Essex, CM7 4SL

Copyright © Miles Kelly Publishing 2002
2 4 6 8 10 9 7 5 3 1

Some material in this book can also be found in *100 Things You Should Know About Birds.*

Editor: Amanda Learmonth

Design: Debbie Meekcoms

Assistant Editor: Nicola Sail

Index: Lynn Bresler

All right reserved. No part of this publication may be reproduced, stored in a retrieval system, or transmitted by any means, electronic, mechanical, photocopying, recording or otherwise, without the prior permission of the copyright holder.

British Library Cataloguing-in-Publication Data
A catalogue record for this book is available from the British Library

ISBN 1-84236-108-2

Printed in Hong Kong

www.mileskelly.net
info@mileskelly.net

ACKNOWLEDGEMENTS

The Publishers would like to thank the following artists who have contributed to this book:

Chris Buzer (Studio Galante), Luca di Castro (Studio Galante), Jim Channell (Bernard Thornton Illustration), Mike Foster (Maltings Partnership), L.R. Galante (Studio Galante), Terry Gabbey (AFA), Roger Gorringe, Brooks Hagan (Studio Galante), Alan Harris, Roger Kent, Kevin Maddison, Janos Marffy, Massimiliano Maugeri (Studio Galante), Eric Robson (Illustration Ltd), Francesco Spadoni (Studio Galante), Rudi Vizi, Mike White (Temple Rogers)

Computer-generated artwork by James Evans

Contents

Birds everywhere **4**

The bird world **6**

Biggest and smallest **8**

Fast fliers **10**

Swimmers and divers **12**

Showing off **14**

Night birds **16**

Bird homes **18**

Flying away **20**

Keep away! **22**

Starting life **24**

Fierce hunters **26**

Family life **28**

Rainforest life **30**

Snow birds **32**

Finding food **34**

River life **36**

Birds and people **38**

Index **40**

Birds everywhere

A bird has two legs, a pair of wings and a body that is covered with feathers. Birds are, perhaps, the animals we see most often in the wild. They live all over the world – everywhere from Antarctica to the hottest deserts and rainforests.

Osprey

Greater flamingo

Grey heron

Mallard

Kingfisher

Birds

Greater honeyguide

Helmeted hornbill

Masai ostrich

Lesser green broadbill

Red-billed hornbill

Blue peafowl

African jacana

Blue-crowned hanging parrot

The greater flamingo uses its beak to filter food from shallow water.

The ostrich has strong legs for fast running.

A hornbill has a horn-like growth on its beak called a casque.

5

The bird world

There are more than 9000 different types, or species, of bird. These have been organized by scientists into groups called orders, which contain many different species. The largest order is called the passerines, also known as perching or song birds. These include common birds such as robins.

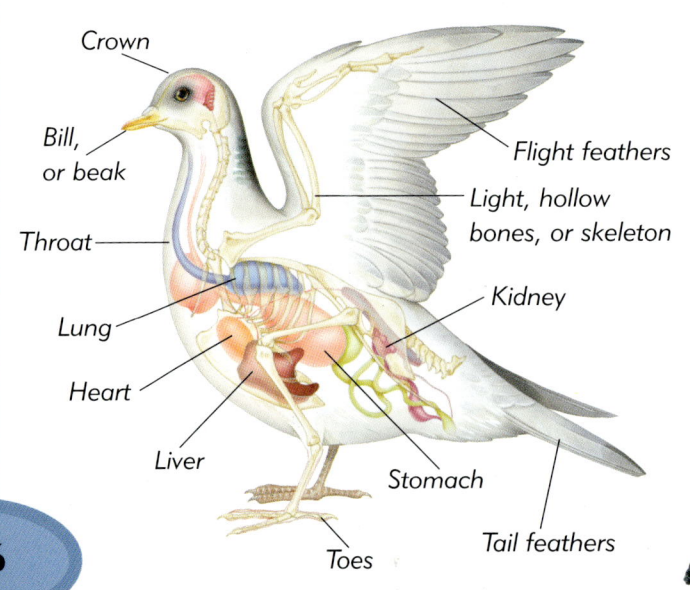

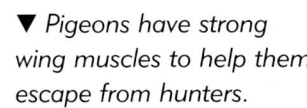

▼ Pigeons have strong wing muscles to help them escape from hunters.

Birds

The goshawk is a hunting bird, or bird of prey. It can kill an animal as big as a rabbit.

The whistling swan is thought to have the most feathers – more than 25,000.

▲ All birds lay eggs. The egg protects the growing young. The parent birds, such as this song thrush, keep the egg safe and warm.

Peggy's fun facts!

Bird brains aren't stupid – ravens and pigeons can work out simple sums, while parrots can copy human speech!

Biggest and smallest

The world's largest bird is the ostrich. It stands up to 2.75 metres tall and weighs up to 115 kilograms – twice as much as an average adult human. The smallest bird is the tiny bee hummingbird, which is only about five centimetres long – scarcely bigger than a real bee.

▼ Ostriches live in the grasslands of Africa, where they feed on leaves, flowers and seeds.

Birds

▲ The wandering albatross has the longest wings of any bird. When outstretched, they measure as much as 3.3 metres from tip to tip.

The bee hummingbird feeds on flower nectar, as do other hummingbirds.

The Andean condor is the biggest type of vulture.

The collared falconet is the smallest bird of prey.

Test your memory!

1. How many types of bird are there?
2. What is the horn-like growth on a hornbill's beak called?
3. What is the largest order of birds called?
4. What is another name for a hunting bird?

Answers: 1. more than 9000 2. a casque 3. the passerines 4. a bird of prey

Fast fliers

The fastest flying bird is the peregrine falcon. It hunts other birds in the air and makes amazing high-speed dives to catch its prey. Ducks and geese are also fast fliers. Many of them, such as the eider duck, can fly at speeds of over 65 kilometres an hour.

Birds

Feed the birds!

In winter, there is not much food for birds. You can make your own food cake to help them.

You will need:
225g of suet, lard or dripping
500g of seeds, nuts, biscuit crumbs and other scraps.

1. Ask an adult for help. Melt the fat, and mix it with the seed and scraps.
2. Pour the mixture into an old yogurt pot (or similar container) and leave it to cool and harden.
3. Remove the cake from the pot. Make a hole through the cake and put a string through the hole. Hang it from a tree outside.

Hummingbirds beat their wings more than 50 times a second as they hover in the air.

Mergansers are ducks which can dive very quickly into the water to catch fish.

Swallows twist and zigzag in the air as they fly.

▲ The swift spends most of its life in the air.

▶ The greater roadrunner is a fast mover on land. It can fly but seems to prefer running!

Swimmers and divers

Penguins are the best swimmers and divers in the bird world. They live in and around the Antarctic, an icy place at the very south of the world. They spend most of their lives in water, using their wings as strong flippers to help them swim.

Emperor penguin

Birds

◀ There are about eighteen different kinds of penguin. Most live in and around the Antarctic.

Northern gannet

The emperor penguin regularly dives deeper than 250 metres.

The northern gannet dives from a great height to catch fish from the sea.

Peggy's fun facts!

The gentoo penguin is one of the fastest swimming birds. It can swim faster than most people can run!

Showing off

Before starting a family, male birds have to attract a female mate. Some do this by showing off their beautiful feathers. Others perform special displays or 'courtship' dances. The male peacock spreads his tail of colourful feathers. He dances up and down and shivers the feathers to get the females' attention.

Peggy's fun facts!

Water birds called great crested grebes offer each other gifts during their 'courtship' dance – beakfuls of water weed!

Birds

▼ Female peacocks tend to choose the males with the most attractive feathers.

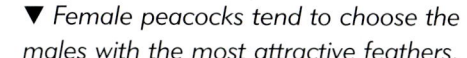

The male cock-of-the-rock does a dance to attract females.

The blue bird of paradise hangs upside-down to show off his feathers.

The male bowerbird builds a twig structure called a bower to impress the females.

Night birds

Some birds hunt insects at night, when there is less competition for prey. These birds have special ways of finding their way in the dark. They might have a strong sense of smell or very sensitive eyesight.

▶ *The kiwi has a good sense of smell, which helps it to find food at night.*

▼ *The kakapo, from New Zealand, is the only parrot that is active at night.*

Kakapo

Birds

Test your memory!

1. What is the world's largest bird?
2. Which bird is the fastest flyer?
3. What kind of bird is a merganser?
4. Which bird builds a nest called a bower?

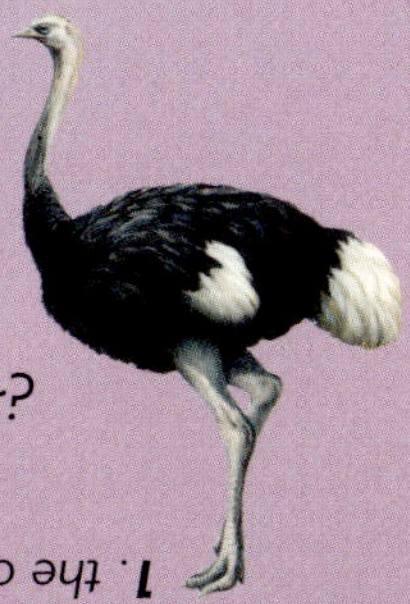

1. the ostrich 2. the peregrine falcon 3. a duck 4. the bowerbird

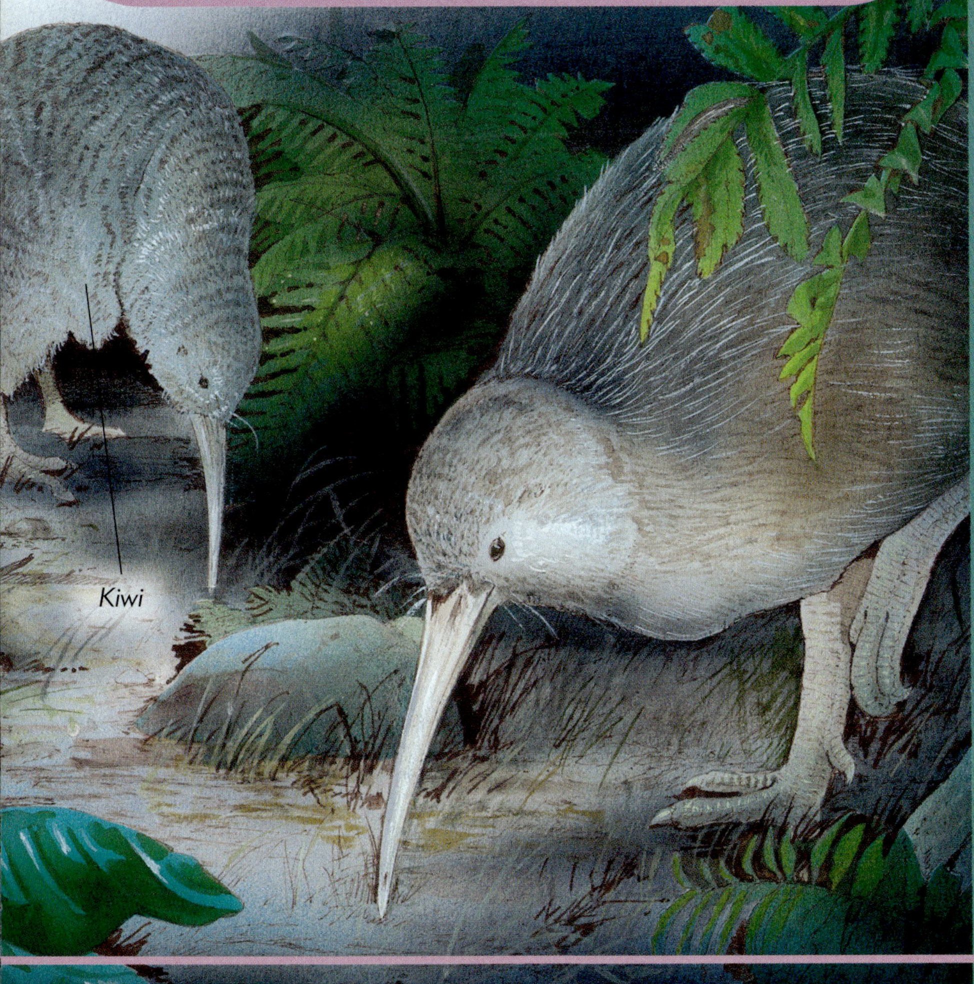

The poorwill hunts at night by opening its beak wide to snap insects out of the air.

The barn owl has large, sensitive eyes to help it see in the dark.

The oilbird uses clicking sounds to help it find its way in the dark.

Kiwi

17

Bird homes

Birds make nests in which to lay their eggs and keep them safe. Nests can be made of twigs, leaves, mud or even saliva or spit. They are built in a variety of places, such as in trees, beside the water or in the walls of buildings.

▶ The bald eagle makes one of the biggest nests of any bird. It is made of sticks and built in a tree or on rocks.

Peggy's fun facts!

Sometimes people collect the nests of cave swiftlets to make bird's nest soup!

Birds

▲ The mallee fowl makes a nest mound made of plants covered with sand. If the mound cools, the male bird adds more sand. If it gets too hot, he makes some holes to let warmth out.

A weaver bird twists strips of leaves around a branch to make its nest.

A cuckoo lays her eggs in the nests of other birds.

The cave swiftlet makes a nest from its own saliva or spit.

19

Flying away

When the weather gets cold, many birds migrate. This means they leave to fly to warmer countries. Here, the birds will find food to eat while they lay their eggs and raise their young.

▼ The Canada goose spends the summer in the Arctic and the winter in North America.

▶ The Arctic tern travels further than any other bird. Every autumn, it flies from the top of the world, the Arctic, to the bottom, the Antarctic.

▲ When birds migrate, they often fly together in a V-shape.

Birds

▲ The American golden plover flies from northern Canada to South America in winter.

Canada geese make loud, honking calls as they fly.

The American golden plover nests in the tundra, a cold Arctic region.

The Arctic tern sees more daylight than any other creature.

Who goes where?

On this world map are the migration routes of the Canada goose, the Arctic tern and the American golden plover. Each one is a different colour. Can you work out which is which?

Blue: Canada goose
Red: Arctic tern
Green: American golden plover

21

Keep away!

Birds have clever ways of protecting themselves from enemies. Some use camouflage, or disguise. This is when the colour and pattern of their feathers blends in with their surroundings, so that they cannot be seen.

Other birds, such as guillemots, live together in large groups for safety.

Birds

The cream-coloured courser is well hidden in its desert surroundings.

The frogmouth disguises itself to look like a branch or tree stump.

▲ Thousands of guillemots live together on cliff tops. They lay their eggs straight on to the rock. Any flying egg thieves are soon driven away by the mass of screeching birds.

Peggy's fun facts!

The guillemot's egg is pear-shaped, so that if the egg is pushed or knocked, it does not fall off the cliff.

Starting life

A bird's egg protects the chick growing inside. The yellow yolk in the egg provides the baby bird with food. Layers of egg white, called albumen, cushion the chick. The hard shell keeps the chick safe. The shell is porous – it allows air in and out so that the chick can breathe. The parent birds keep the egg warm in a nest. This is called incubation.

▶ The ostrich egg is the biggest in the world. This is its actual size!

▶ This is a life-size picture of a bee hummingbird egg. It is the smallest egg in the world.

Birds

Test your memory!

1. What is the name of the parrot that is active at night?
2. Which bird makes the biggest nest?
3. What is the word used to describe the journey that birds take when they fly to warmer places?
4. Where do guillemots live?

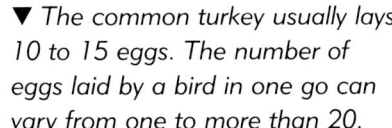

Answers: 1. the kakapo 2. the bald eagle 3. migration 4. on cliff tops

Step 1
The chick uses its egg tooth to chip away at the eggshell.

Step 2
The egg splits wide open.

Step 3
The chick is able to wriggle free.

▼ The common turkey usually lays 10 to 15 eggs. The number of eggs laid by a bird in one go can vary from one to more than 20.

25

Fierce hunters

Eagles, hawks and owls are all birds of prey. These are birds who hunt other animals. The golden eagle is one of the fiercest of all birds of prey. When it spies a victim, it dives down and seizes its prey in its powerful claws, called talons.

Word scramble

Unscramble these words to find the names of four different birds of prey:

1. GALEE
2. KHAW
3. LOW
4. NEARV

1. EAGLE 2. HAWK 3. OWL 4. RAVEN

Birds

▼ The golden eagle can soar for hours on its huge wings, searching for prey such as rabbits, birds and mice.

Steller's sea eagle swoops down to the ocean and seizes fish in its sharp claws.

The raven mainly hunts rats and mice, but it can kill larger animals, such as rabbits.

The crested serpent eagle feeds mostly on snakes and lizards.

Family life

Each species of bird has its own way of caring for its young. Emperor penguins lay eggs and rear (bring up) their young on the Antarctic ice. Hawks and falcons look after their young and bring them food for many weeks. Other birds, such as ducks and geese, are able to run around and find food as soon as they hatch.

Birds

▼ *While the male penguin incubates the egg (keeps it warm), he does not eat. When the chick hatches, the female returns to take over its care.*

◀ *A female mallard leads her ducklings in the water.*

Swans carry their young, called cygnets, on their back as they swim.

Sparrowhawks are born blind and helpless, so need their parents' care for many weeks.

Peggy's fun facts!

Penguins huddle together for warmth while they incubate their eggs. They take it in turns to stand on the outside and take the force of the cold winds.

Rainforest life

The rainforests of the world are home to a huge variety of bird life. One-fifth of all the kinds of birds in the world live in the Amazon rainforest, in South America. Birds of paradise are among the most colourful of all birds. They live in the rainforests of New Guinea and Australia.

Harpy eagle

Hoatzin

Congo peafowl

Birds

Test your memory!

1. What part of an egg is the albumen?
2. What is the smallest bird's egg in the world?
3. What are the claws of a bird of prey called?
4. Which bird lays its egg on Antarctic ice?

1. the egg white 2. the bee hummingbird's egg 3. talons 4. the penguin

The harpy eagle is the world's biggest eagle.

The scarlet macaw is a parrot that lives in South America.

The junglefowl is related to the farmyard chicken.

Quetzal

Scarlet macaw

Junglefowl

31

Snow birds

The coldest places on Earth are the Arctic and the Antarctic. Both places are too cold for most birds to live there all year round. During the Arctic summer, birds nest and feed on ice-free land called the tundra. In the Antarctic, most of the land is covered in ice.

▼ Snowy buntings breed farthest north than any other bird.

Snowy sheathbill

Snowy bunting

Snowy owl

Ptarmigan

▶ The ptarmigan has white feathers to help hide it from enemies among the Arctic snow.

Birds

Chilly quiz

All of the birds in this picture live in the north, the Arctic, except for two. Which two birds live in the south, the Antarctic?

The penguins and the snowy sheathbill are the only birds in this picture that live in the Antarctic.

The snowy owl is the one of the largest Arctic birds.

The snowy sheathbill lives on islands around the Antarctic.

The tundra swan brings up its young in the Arctic tundra.

Emperor penguins

◀ Penguins have a thick layer of fat under their skin to protect them from the cold.

Tundra swan

33

Finding food

Insects, seeds and small creatures are common types of bird food. Some birds have an unusual diet: honeyguides eat bee grubs and honey, while hummingbirds feed on flower nectar.

◀ The woodpecker uses its strong beak to make holes in the tree trunk and catch insects.

Birds

Honey badger

Honeyguide bird

▲ The honeyguide bird uses the honey badger to help it get food. It leads the badger towards the bees' nest. The honey badger smashes into the nest, and the honeyguide eats its fill.

The antbird follows marching army ants around the forest. It eats the insects that try to escape from the ants.

Hummingbirds sip flower nectar using their long tongue.

Peggy's fun facts!

Honeyguide birds have been known to lead honey-loving humans to bees' nests.

River life

Rivers, lakes and marshes are a favourite habitat, or home, for birds. There are plenty of fish, insects and plants to eat and places to nest. Herons, ducks and geese are commonly found in watery places, as well as kingfishers and pelicans.

▶ The dipper is a small bird that lives around fast-flowing streams. It walks along the bottom of the stream, snapping up insects.

Birds

Test your memory!

1. Which is the biggest eagle in the world?
2. What kind of bird is a scarlet macaw?
3. Where does the snowy owl live?
4. What do hummingbirds feed on?

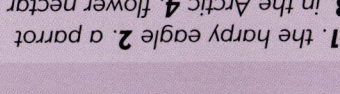

1. the harpy eagle 2. a parrot 3. in the Arctic 4. flower nectar

The kingfisher hunts fish along streams and riverbanks.

The heron stands in shallow water and grabs its prey with its sharp beak.

The jacana has long toes that allow it to walk on floating lily pads.

Birds and people

Many kinds of birds are now endangered species. This means that they are in danger of dying out. The parrot family was once common in the rainforests. Now many parrots are rare, as people have been stealing them from the wild to sell.

▶ Starlings are very common city birds. They can eat many foods and nest almost anywhere.

Birds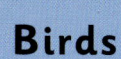

Parrots are taken from the wild to be put in cages and sold as pets.

Chickens are reared for their meat and eggs.

Peggy's fun facts!

Sometimes crows place walnuts in front of cars. The cars move over the nuts, breaking the shells for them to eat!

Index

A B C
albatross, wandering **9**
Antarctic 12, 13, 32–33
antbird **35**
Arctic 20–21, 32
bird of paradise **15**, 30
birds of prey **7**, **9**, 26–27
bowerbird **15**
bunting, snowy **32**
camouflage 22
chicken **39**
chicks 24, **25**
cock-of-the-rock **15**
condor, Andean **9**
courser,
    cream-coloured **23**
crow **39**
cuckoo **19**
cygnets **29**

D E F
dipper **36–37**
ducks 10, 11, 28–29, 36
eagle **26–27**, 31
    bald **18**
    crested serpent **27**
    golden **26–27**
    harpy **30**, 31
    Steller's sea **27**

eggs **7**, **23**, **24–25**, 28, 29
falcon 28
    peregrine **10**
falconet, collared **9**
feathers **4**, **6**, **7**, 14
flamingo, greater **4, 5**
flippers 12
food 34–35
fowl, mallee **19**
frogmouth **23**

G H
gannet, northern **13**
goose, geese 10, 28, 36
    Canada **20, 21**
goshawk **7**
grebe, great crested 14
guillemot **22–23**, 25
hawk 26, 28
heron **4**, 36, **37**
hoatzin **30**
honeyguide **5**, 34, **35**
hornbill,
    helmeted **5**
    red-billed **5**
hummingbird **11**, 34, **35**
    bee 8, **9**, 24

I J K
incubation 24, 29
jacana **5**, **37**
junglefowl **31**

kakapo **16**
kingfisher **4**, 36, **37**
kiwi 16–**17**

M N O
macaw, scarlet **31**
mallard **4**, **28–29**
merganser **11**
migrate, migration 20–21
nests **18–19**, 24
oilbird **17**
orders 6
osprey **4**
ostrich **5**, **8**, 24
owl 26
    barn **17**
    snowy **32**, **33**

P Q
parrot **16**, 38, **39**
    blue-crowned
    hanging **5**
passerines 6
peacock **14–15**
peafowl **5**, **30**
penguin **12–13**, 28, 29, 33
    emperor **12**, **13**, 28
    gentoo 13
pigeon **6–7**
plover, American

    golden **21**
poorwill **17**
ptarmigan **32**
quetzal **31**

R S
rainforests 30–31, 38
raven 7, **27**
roadrunner, greater **11**
robins 6, **9**
sheathbill, snowy **32**, **33**
sparrowhawk **29**
starling **38–39**
swallow **11**
swan **29**
    tundra **33**
    whistling **7**
swift **11**
swiftlet, cave 18, **19**

T V W
talons 26, 37
tern, Arctic **20**, **21**
thrush, song **7**
tundra 32, 33
turkey, common **25**
vulture **9**
weaver bird **19**
wings 9, 11, 12
woodpecker **34**